AMERICAN ARTISTS
in the American Ambassador's
Residence *in* Paris

AMERICAN ARTISTS
in the American Ambassador's Residence *in* Paris

Foreword by Felix Rohatyn, *American Ambassador*
41, Rue du Faubourg Saint-Honoré, Paris VIIIe

Coordinated by Jeanne Greenberg Art Advisory

4

TABLE OF CONTENTS

JACOB LAWRENCE
Library III, 1960
Tempera on board.
29 x 23½ inches

Opposite:
The Ambassador and
Mrs. Felix Rohatyn,
with *Avenue of the
Allies,* Childe Hassam,
1926.

To TENS OF THOUSANDS of French men and women this Residence is an important symbol of America's relationship with France. Its elegance, its majesty, its location, all contribute to making the American Ambassador's Residence one of the showplaces in Paris.

When President Clinton honored me with this appointment, my wife and I felt we could add a dimension to the Residence by showcasing American modern and contemporary art. There are few countries in the world more sensitive to cultural issues than France. By selecting works of twentieth century American artists who lived and worked in France or who were deeply influenced by French art, we believe that we can bring attention to a cultural link between our two countries that may not have been self evident.

We also believe that by exhibiting these American artists at the Residence, we would show that all of America recognizes their great contribution to art history.

We are immensely grateful to the artists, galleries, and museums who contributed their works to this endeavor. We are proud to be associated with it and are most appreciative of the work of the Art in Embassies Program and Jeanne Greenberg Art Advisory in bringing it about.

We trust that this initiative will provide not only aesthetic pleasure to our many friends and visitors, but a better understanding of the deep and varied cultural ties between our two countries.

Felix Rohatyn   *Elizabeth Rohatyn*

ELLSWORTH KELLY
Fête à Torcy, 1952
Oil on canvas, two panels.
45½ x 38 inches

THE LOUIS XVI SALON The gold leaf
in this salon was restored after a workman
discovered it under a coat of paint in 1971.
Period furnishings include a Louis XVI
mahogany side table with molded and turned
tapered legs decorated with spiral brass
beading. A pair of Regency giltwood
console tables have serpentine Breche
d'Alep marble tops above foliated supports
and cartouches. A Louis XVI gilt bronze
"geographic" clock by Cresp is on the Louis
XV Rouge Languedoc marble mantelpiece.
The French Empire chandelier has
thirty-two arms stretching from a gilded
bronze frame.

Roy Lichtenstein
Paintings: Picasso Head, 1984
Oil and magna on canvas.
64 x 70 inches

THE JEFFERSON CABINET ROOM
The oak-paneled library was inaugurated
in July 1996 as the Jefferson Cabinet Room.
Named after the study in Monticello, where
Jefferson used to read and write, this room
holds two book collections which once
belonged to William Short, the personal
secretary to Thomas Jefferson during his
tenure as Ambassador to France between
1785 and 1789. The collection includes
a set of ninety-two Rousseau volumes
with jaspé flyleaf dated 1785 and a set of
twenty-one Voltaire volumes with marbleized
flyleaf dated 1818.

Under the German occupation the room
was a Luftwaffe officer's bar. The Louis XIV
oak panels were covered at that time with
heavy geometric carved panels. These older
panels were discovered during the 1966-
1972 restoration.

BRICE MARDEN
Couplet IV, 1988-89
Oil on linen. 108 x 60 inches

JOSEPH CORNELL
Untitled (Grand Hôtel Bon Port)
circa 1950-59. Mixed media box
construction. 18⅞ x 12 x 4⅛ inches

THE SAMUEL BERNARD SALON
Thanks to its elegant proportions and
detailed wall treatments this central salon is
one of unusual splendor. Named after
Jacques-Samuel Bernard, from whom Baron
de Rothschild purchased the paneling, this
room is designed in the style of Louis XV.
Samuel Bernard's salon had ornate moldings
depicting eagles and *putti*, sculpted
allegorical figures representing the arts, and
canvases over the doors painted by Van Loo,
Natoire, Restout and Dumaret. These panels
were donated by Mauric de Rothschild to
the Israel Museum in Jerusalem. The panels
in the room today are plaster facsimiles.

The salon is furnished with four giltwood
Transition period armchairs signed by
J.B. Cresson, cabinetmaker to Louis XV, a
pair of commodes by Jacob Coulon, and,
on the mantle, a rare bronze elephant clock
by Henri Voisin.

Robert Rosenblum

BORN AND RAISED in Manhattan, I spent the 1940s immersing myself in the faith of a new kind of art, as propagated in its shrine on West 53rd Street. Everything I learned at the Museum of Modern Art about the audacious look and feel that seemed to belong to our century alone had its roots, I thought, somewhere in Paris, whether in the labyrinthine complexities of Picasso's Cubism, the aerodynamic sleekness of Brancusi's birds, or the geometric purities of Le Corbusier's gravity-defiant houses. And then in 1950, thanks to a Fullbright Grant, the reality of Paris suddenly lay before me. I was given a year to study art history in the city that nurtured my New Yorker's vision of a Brave New Visual World.

It was a crushing disappointment. Like other Americans I was of course totally enchanted by my first view of a city whose streets had names rather than numbers, whose architecture went way back before our Civil War, and whose restaurants offered such then unfamiliar treats as crudités and quiches, which were clearly superior to our luncheon choices back home. But where, oh where, was the city of modern art I had dreamed of? I of course rushed to Paris's equivalent of New York's MoMA, the Musée de'Art Moderne; but compared to what I grew up with, this might almost have been Versailles. The architecture itself, in somewhat derelict condition, conformed to what Henry-Rusell Hitchcock once wittily characterized as "le style Louis xx," that is, a 20th-century hybrid of traditional classical composition and stripped geometric decoration that evoked ancient grandeur, not the factories and airplanes I had been taught expressed the contemporary spirit; and the museum's holdings revealed a comparable conservatism in which the occasional appearance, of say, a Matisse or a Braque *papier collé* was vastly overwhelmed by reactionary French artists whose names I then barely knew—Marcel Gromaire, André Dunoyer de Segonzac, Roger Chapdelain-Midi, André Marchand. This was so far from the metallic, gleaming vision of art and life's future that had nurtured me in New York that I felt immediately homesick for the religion of modernism; and as I recall it, the only flashes I found of my New York idea of contemporary modernity turned up in the Paris branch of Knoll International Furniture.

Training to be an art historian, I of course did lots of homework in the mythic land that had been mapped out for me on 53rd Street. I visited Brancusi's atelier in the Impasse Ronsin; I trekked out to Neuilly to see the paintings left to Kandinsky's widow, Nina; I got myself invited to an evening chez Alice B. Toklas on the Rue Christine, where I was admittedly more riveted by Ms. Toklas's odd appearance and beautiful English than by Gertrude Stein's old Picassos; and I even once touched base with an old American expatriate, Man Ray, whose baguette painted a brilliant blue was the most unforgettable of the loony objects that littered his studio. But these fragments of modern art all seemed hidden time-capsules to me, early twentieth-century artifacts I had to excavate from under the oppressive weight of the French tradition. I wanted modern art to be the very air one breathed, not archaeology.

As for the air, Americans in 1950 had begun to notice that, right from their very soil, a strange new painting was developing that might well deflect the course of modern art from its historic center in Paris to a distant city unshackled by traditions, New York. I had already had my sense of modern art's future through early sightings of the puzzling but invigorating canvases of Jackson Pollock and Willem de Kooning, of Mark Rothko and Clyfford Still; and my instinct that Paris could no longer hatch artists who would make a real difference was early confirmed by America's most influential critic, Clement Greenberg, who, in 1947, writing about an exhibition at the Whitney Museum, "Painting in France, 1939-46," asserted that however charming these French artists might be, they couldn't compare to their American contemporaries in terms of originality, honesty, and force. It was certainly the way I felt; and when I returned to New York in 1951, after my Fulbright year in Paris, I thought I had been catapulted from the comforting seductions of an irrelevant French past to the rugged, future oriented energy of those American rebels who wanted to slam the door on history and start from scratch.

By the next decade, in fact, this transatlantic upheaval already seemed to be certified aesthetic truth. New York painting, we all believed, *was* better than its French counterparts; and familiar comparisons —Pierre Soulages versus Franz Kline, Bram van Velde versus Willem de Kooning, Jackson Pollock versus Georges Mathieu—were often made in order to demonstrate the muscular power and originality of the American product vis-à-vis the old-fashioned refinements of the French look-alikes. Aesthetic patriotism is hardly a noble cause, but there is no doubt that most Americans who cared about what was vital in new art had an absolute faith that from 1945 on, what would matter was going to happen in New York and not in Paris.

This strong prejudice, which I fully shared, had its antagonistic corollary in Paris, where the work of one American generation of artists after another was received with relative indifference or downright hostility. My own life and professional work (which now veered toward the study of French art from the late eighteenth century) kept me an annual and often semi-annual visitor to Paris, where I would totally ignore contemporary art except for what was being exported from New York. I particularly remember the early 1960s when, one by one, an older or a younger American master I admired would make what seemed a stealthy appearance in a Paris museum or gallery, only to disappear again. I recall, for one, the major Rothko show from MoMA that was imported to Paris in the winter of 1962-63 and turned out to be a non-event, with barely a soul in the galleries, except for some expatriates like me who thirsted for visual nourishment from back home. And in the early 1960s, several enterprising New York dealers, Ileana Sonnabend and Lawrence Rubin, opened Parisian outposts that would feature the latest news from younger American generations. There, at the Galerie Sonnabend in 1963, the 1962 shock of Roy Lichtenstein's Pop art was sent off to Paris, where nobody but me and a few others seemed to notice it. And soon after, in 1964, I was able to confirm my New York-based excitement about Andy Warhol and Frank Stella by seeing their shows at the Galerie Sonnabend and the Galerie Lawrence, where, typically, the audience consisted of that small circle of American fans who happened to be living in or passing through Paris. These events, the latest headlines from the American front, seemed to take place in a sealed-off world that barely made a ripple in Paris but that made Americans like me homesick for the raw, tough audacity of life and art back in New York. I remember thinking that if I wanted to live where the action was, I'd better get back to my roots.

I offer these personal reminiscences about the long Cold War between the French and American art worlds that began just before my first series of sojourns in Paris because the situation, I'm happy to say, is totally different today and has been since the 1980s. This was confirmed once again not only by my first visit in January 1998 to see the collection assembled for the new American ambassador's residence in Paris, but by two more casual observations about the present state of Franco-American art relations gleaned at the same time. Just after visiting the ambassador's collection, I happened to travel to the Musée des Beaux-Arts in Rouen. There I noticed a poster for an exhibition of work by Joan Mitchell, an artist who had first forged her career in the New York of the 1950s as a highly individual disciple of de Kooning, but who then moved to France in 1959, and then, in 1967, left Paris for Vétheuil, where she remained until her death in 1992. Vétheuil, of course, was a site famous in the history of French Impressionism, for it was there, between 1878 and 1881, that Monet had painted every conceivable nuance of the four seasons and rapidly changing skies of Normandie. The work of Mitchell's last decades, in fact, offers a ravishing marriage of these Monet memories with her New York school foundations. Who now would want to split her art in two, as a war between America and France? And wasn't it the most natural of public events that Normandie's major museum would honor this American expatriate, much as in its own permanent collection it honored the reverse side of this Franco-American discourse, namely, the work of its native son, Marcel Duchamp, who early gave up France in order to flourish more freely in New York? And still in Rouen, while visiting the museum's bookshop, I noticed a brand-new exhibition catalogue from Nice's Musée d'Art Moderne et Contemporaine. As its title proclaimed (*De Klein à Warhol; face à face France/États-Unis* [From Klein to Warhol: France/United States Encounter]), this show traced the ongoing dialogue between French and American artists from the 1950s on, not in a spirit of combat, but of friendly interchange of transatlantic ideas.

Such a pair of accidental observations in Rouen reinforced my sense at the ambassador's residence that the Cold War I had lived through was now only a memory carried by people of my generation. The collection itself gave ample proof of counter-traditions of the most peaceful Franco-American dialogue. That theme was perhaps launched most startlingly by an immense canvas, more than 15 feet high, of an equestrian ruler who presides over the grand stair the way a portrait of Louis XIV on horseback might dominate the stairwell of a seventeenth-century chateau. But appropriately enough for this diplomatic setting, the venerable horseman can be immediately recognized as George Washington, although it was no less clear that this huge painting was skillful and imposing enough to have been painted for a Bourbon or Napoleonic ruler. Indeed, it turned out to be the work of a highly polished and successful French painter, René Princeteau (1844-1914), who had labored on this canvas in 1875-76 in his atelier at 243 Rue du Faubourg St. Honoré, by coincidence only a short walk west of the current ambassador's home. Moreover, the painting was made to be shown at the Philadelphia Centennial International Exhibition of 1876 as a French tribute to the father of the American nation. What better symbol could anchor the continuing dialogue between the two countries that is borne out in the later works of these ambassadorial walls?

For one, there is in the Blue Room a trio of small paintings by that archetypal American artist Edward Hopper which suddenly reminds us that this yankee, whose images of barren, silent spaces and lonely people have become an international symbol for American emptiness and isolation, owed a good part of his youthful formation to Paris. On two visits there, in 1906-07 and in 1909, he recorded, in the Impressionist tradition, casual and oblique glimpses of the city, especially views along the Seine—a laundry, a riverboat, the turn of a quai. Yet these urban vignettes, from the core of what was reputed to be the most cheerful and socially animated city of the world, already speak with the artist's American accent, translating Paris into a domain of cold light and unpopulated spaces that have their root in Main Street, USA. In contrast, an older American painter, Childe Hassam, in another Blue Room painting, could Frenchify New York City. Learning the essential components of his art in France between 1886 and 1889, he used these lessons, especially those learned from the Impressionists, to depict American city and country scenes. The climax of his career might be considered a series of paintings he did in 1917-18 of the jingoistic pageantry prompted by America's intervention in the First World War. These sunshot, vibrant views of American and foreign flags merging with milling crowds along Fifth Avenue (then called "Avenue of the Allies") stem from Hassam's earlier effort to depict a scene of chauvinistic flag-waving in Paris rather than New York, namely a 1910 view of the Rue Danou bedecked with the tricolor on Bastille Day. And this painting in turn goes back to French prototypes by Manet and Monet, who launched this nationalistic theme way back in the 1870s, a theme that would later be resurrected by Jasper Johns in the 1950s, when, as in the 1958 version of Old Glory in the ambassador's collection, a brash, America First salute to the stars and stripes is relocated in a Duchampian enigma of fact versus fiction, common object versus aesthetic meditation.

As a completely different kind of transatlantic dialogue, the collection offers some of the earliest works of Louise Bourgeois, a sculptor of growing international prominence whose personal background is a dense mix of Franco-American liaisons. Born in Paris in 1911, she was married in 1938 to a distinguished American art historian, Robert Goldwater, and then settled in New York where she worked with such Parisian artists in exile as Joan Miró and André Masson, whose Surrealist influence is apparent on her cluster of totemic sculptures from the years 1947-51 that burgeon surprisingly in the corner of the Samuel Bernard Salon. Who would want to impose a French or American passport on this art? In aesthetic as well as autobiographical terms, it belongs to both worlds. So, too, does Ellsworth Kelly's *Fête à Torcy,* painted in 1952 toward the end of the American artist's six-year sojourn in France. Its title alludes to the perplexed response to the painting by a villager at Torcy, on the Marne, where Kelly was then living. Anticipating the arrival of representatives of the Galerie Maeght, who were coming to see his work, the artist hung the canvas outside his villa, Les Charmettes, on a wall alongside the road. Passing by this surprising spectacle, a puzzled farmer's son asked his father "qu'est-ce que c'est que ça Papa?" [what is that, Papa?], to which the answer was "pour la Fête à Torcy" [for the village's summer festival]. His sense of the work's chromatic power, however, was not off the mark; for the work does recall Le Corbusier's *Unité d'Habitation* in Marseilles, whose slabs of primary color had impressed Kelly when he visited the architect's just-completed masterpiece earlier that year.

In fact, such happy intermarriages can be spotted throughout the ambassadorial residence, at least if one thinks of the art world in terms of a see-sawing balance between Paris and New York: Roy Lichtenstein's large 1984 painting in a small room (The Jefferson Cabinet) presents the artist's familiar quotations from art history, in this case offering, as in an Olympic showdown, the leader of rebellious Parisian modernism, Picasso (represented by a generic Dora Maar head), vis-à-vis the leader of the New York School, De Kooning (represented by a generic abstract "action painting" that, ironically, closely resembles the real De Kooning that now hangs in the ambassador's ballroom and dates from the previous year, 1983). But for really distant Franco-American time travel, nothing beats Cindy Sherman's porcelain tea set, in which the artist, known for donning the face and clothing of everyone from 1940s Hollywood starlets to John Singleton Copley's Bostonian ladies, recreates herself in a role of the ultimate French artifice, that of Mme de Pompadour, whose luxurious presence adorns the spectacular neo-Rococo tea service. This 1990s revival of the most ornate style of the eighteenth century offers an unexpected echo of the art historical appropriations found in the ambassador's residence itself, which, like so many French buildings of the second half of the nineteenth century, nostalgically mirrors, in the heyday of industrialization, the handmade, aristocratic decoration associated with the lost world of the *ancien régime.* We might well have expected nineteenth-century French architects and interior designers to evoke the Rococo as a theatrical dream of history, but it may come as a surprise that a younger New York artist can resurrect, at the end of our own century, this privileged society of exquisite craftsmanship and quicksilver animation.

Fascinating, too, is the way the neo-Rococo interiors of the ambassador's residence, so overtly French in character, can provide harmonious framing elements for American paintings that one might at first consider totally alien to these symbols of venerable French culture. But in fact, these interiors can provide visual hospitality to everything from Brice Marden's fragile webs of meandering abstract lines to a classic flag image by Jasper Johns, which lets us know, in no uncertain terms, that a vigorous American presence is in the heart of Paris. Long may its red, white, and blue wave together with the French tricolor!

Georgia O'Keeffe
Yellow Calla, 1926
Oil on fiberboard. 9⅜ x 12¾ inches

Arthur Dove
Broome County From the Black
Diamond, 1931-32
Oil on canvas. 18¼ x 24 inches

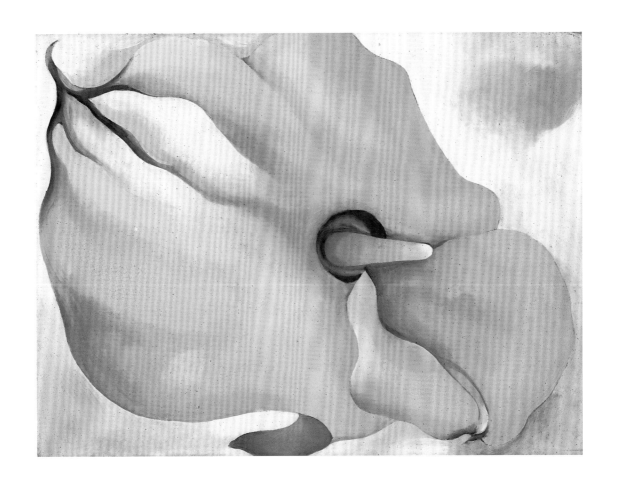

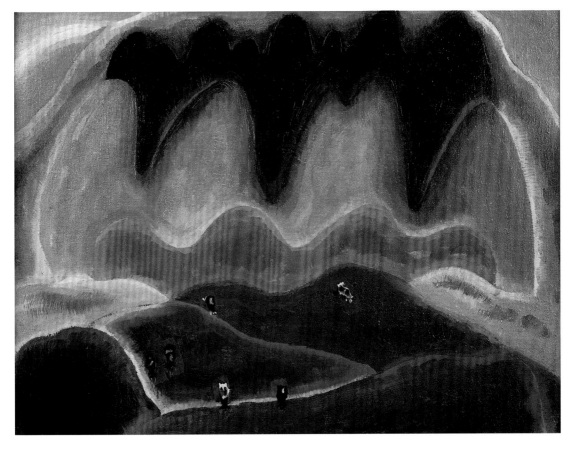

CHILDE HASSAM
Avenue of the Allies, 1917
Oil on canvas. 18⅛ x 15⅛ inches

THE BLUE ROOM This is the first of
three salons which the architect Felix
Langlais decorated in the styles of Louis XIV,
XV, and XVI respectively. This intimate room
seems eminently suited to its present role as
a gallery for artworks. Deep blue fabric
covers the walls, which once held Chinese
lacquered panels. These panels have been
recently restored by French artisans and will
soon be reinstalled.

A rare Louis XVI parquetry writing table
stands to the left of the mantelpiece, along
with a Louis XVI mahogany *rafraîchissoir*,
in the style of the cabinetmaker Canabas.
Between the windows is a French transitional
tulipwood parquetry commode with a
Breche d'Alep marble top.

ELLSWORTH KELLY
Chatham V, 1971
Oil on canvas, two panels.
108 x 99 inches

THE BALLROOM Once used by the Luftwaffe
as a theatre, the most spacious room in the
east wing has been restored to its original
purpose as a ballroom [furthest room
pictured, opposite]. Concerts, lectures, and
films are now enjoyed in this room. A
projection room is behind a large portrait of
George Washington painted by Charles
Wilson Peale (1741-1827). Oak panels in
the ballroom, sculpted in 1740 for the
Jacques-Samuel Bernard residence, show
scenes from the *Fables* of Jean de La Fontaine
(1621-1695).

The original paintwork of the Louis xv
panels was stripped during the Rothschild
era, but repainted in 1984. The Belgian
red-marble mantelpiece was originally in
the Samuel Bernard Salon.

MAURICE PRENDERGAST
Beach Scene #4, 1903-06
Oil on panel. 10⅜ x 13⅝ inches

MAURICE PRENDERGAST
Maine, Blue Hills, 1907-10
Oil on panel. 10⅜ x 13¾ inches

And so I am an American and I have lived half my life in Paris, not the half that made me but the half in which I made what I made. —Gertrude Stein, "An American and France," 1940

Michael Plante

AMERICAN PAINTER JOAN MITCHELL felt a sense of shock and disillusionment when she arrived in France in the spring of 1948 after a ten-day ocean journey: "Arriving in Le Havre on that Liberty ship and seeing all those … ships sunk. … I mean, war, war, war, war. … Everything rationed, and the poor people … I mean, we didn't suffer like that."[1] This was the shorter of her two stays in France, and the level of deprivation and destruction suffered by the French during the war was incomprehensible to her. The French exiles who spent the war years in New York were similarly horrified. One of the few Americans who realized the desperation of French life during and after the occupation of German troops was Baroness Hilla Rebay, director of the Museum of Non-Objective Painting (later, the Solomon R. Guggenheim Museum of Art), who continually sent packages of clothes and food to her friends. As late as the spring of 1947 Rebay was still sending packages to artists such as Albert Gleizes and Sonia and Robert Delaunay.[2] In the minds of most Americans Paris was still very much the center of the art world, and certainly it revived after 1947. But Paris would never regain the standard it held in the Golden Age, a period when American collectors, writers, and artists seemed so important to the cultural life of the city, even as they attempted to communicate that verve to America's intelligentsia and, perhaps most importantly, to the early American collectors of modern painting.

Opposite top:
EDWARD HOPPER
Le Bistro or The Wine Shop, 1909
Oil on canvas.
23⅜ x 28½ inches

Opposite bottom:
EDWARD HOPPER
Le Quai des Grands Augustins, 1909
Oil on canvas.
23½ x 28½ inches

Americans for the most part were unwilling to admit that Paris, the accepted cultural center of the world, had suffered so much damage, and young Americans continued what amounted to a pilgrimage to the great monuments of modern France, searching for the Paris captured by Gertrude Stein, F. Scott Fitzgerald, and George Gershwin. What little was known of contemporary life in Europe was played out on the silver screen. What the average American knew about the Vichy government had been learned from *Casablanca* (1942). By 1951 American audiences were rushing to see Vincent Minnelli's *An American in Paris*, the story of an American expatriate painter, played by Gene Kelly, who goes to Paris on the G.I. Bill to paint. Through Kelly's costuming, his rapport with his French neighbors, and the narrative organized around the music of George Gershwin (mostly from the 1920s) Hollywood promoted an extremely superficial and conservative view of postwar Paris. Kelly's paintings in the film, done by Gene Grant, were pastiches of early 1920s modernism, closely related to Utrillo and Modigliani, and bore no relation to contemporary artistic production. The movie was filmed on a Hollywood backlot, and only the exteriors were shot in Paris.[3] *An American in Paris* served to fix in the popular American imagination the idea that Paris had not changed during the

Occupation. Gene Kelly's character is a happy-go-lucky expatriate, and the much-heralded ballet sequence of the film features backdrops that recapitulate and reinforce the importance of the French tradition of painting, as scenes from the works of Dufy, Renoir, Utrillo, Rousseau, Van Gogh, and Toulouse-Lautrec come to life. *An American in Paris* won the Academy Award for Best Picture in 1952, which signals the extent to which American audiences were pleased to be presented with this comforting view of Paris. Nowhere did Americans see ordinary French citizens trudging through Paris streets *clopin-clopant*. What had fueled the commitment to the Liberation of Paris was the memory of Paris—its beauty, romance, and cultural avant-gardism—and films such as *An American in Paris* were intended to reassure audiences that Paris was still there, as alive and vibrant as ever.

Paris represented the fountainhead of a sort of modernism which the United States eagerly consumed. The beginnings of American art paralleled the birth of the modern movement in Europe, and although important models were available in England, Germany, and Italy, Americans consistently turned to France to provide examples which they recognized as intellectually advanced, sophisticated, and urban. The transatlantic dialogue at the beginning in the nineteenth-century was little more than a one-way street across the Atlantic. Nevertheless, important Americans would be recognized as contributors to European styles, in particular Mary Cassatt, John Singer Sargent, and James McNeill Whistler. Often, as in the case of American cubism, a misreading of the French style resulted in a unique and different style. Toward the middle of the twentieth century, American painting became less dependent upon French models, and instead began to communicate advanced artistic ideas to Paris, through expatriates and exhibitions of American painting sent abroad.

 Americans with artistic ambition traditionally had flocked to Paris, Munich, or Rome to gain artistic training that was not yet available in the United States. The prerequisite to working in these European cities was participation in the annual salons, which were were never so plentiful as in Paris and which were for American artists a vital part of the expatriate experience. That so many Americans studied in the ateliers of the leading academicians during the late nineteenth century ensured that American artists would be represented at the annual Salons. By the 1890s American artists accounted for twenty to twenty-five percent of all foreign participants in both the Champs-de-Mars and Champs-Elysées Salons; foreign participation totaled approximately fifteen percent of all entries. At the Salon of 1880, the work of 107 American artists was displayed; 177 Americans participated in the Salon of 1890; 234 were included in the Salon of 1899. The large expatriate population of American artists in the last decades of the nineteenth century in Europe made their impression on public French art exhibitions— at the Universal Exposition of 1889, for example, the display of American art was the largest of all the foreign art exhibits. Additionally, paintings by American expatriates, most living in Paris, accounted for twice the number of pictures as those by artists resident in the United States. Though it could be argued that it was far easier to include canvases by expatriate artists than to import canvases from

abroad, this was certainly not a consideration for the 1889 Exposition. Of the awards given to U.S. paintings at the Exposition—2 grand prix, 4 gold medals, and 14 silver medals—all were by "demi-Français," or artists who at some point in their lives had lived, studied, and exhibited in Paris.[4] It was not merely the chance to live in Europe that attracted young American artists but also the opportunity to exhibit their work alongside that of their foreign contemporaries—a chance to gauge their work against that of the best Europeans.

A European education became *de rigeur* for American artists. Childe Hassam left Boston in 1886 for the French capital, largely under the influence of William Morris Hunt, the important patron and disciple of Jean-François Millet and the Barbizon School, which also included Corot, Rousseau, and Daubigny.[5] Like many artists of his generation, Hassam spent an important period (1886–89) training in France, and continued to visit throughout the years he was based in New York City. Maurice Prendergast, another expatriate of the Golden Age, left Boston for France in 1891 and traveled widely throughout Europe, although he remained in Paris until 1894. Though he studied at various ateliers, he was particularly influenced by the Nabis, especially Paul Gauguin and Paul Sérusier, and his work came to be characterized by large crowds of people in parks, on beaches, or on city streets. Prendergast's knowledge of advanced French painting is demonstrated in the flattened composition in *Beach Scene #4*, with its decorative rhythm of paper-thin clouds and figures aligned in rows of bright color.

Importantly, both Hassam and Prendergast would bring their newly formed styles—so dependent upon French modernism—to the United States. In December 1897 Hassam and nine other painters signed a resolution to resign from the Society of American Artists. In 1898 Hassam, along with John H. Twachtman, J. Alden Weir, and others, exhibited work in a show entitled "10 American Painters" after which they were referred to by the nickname "The Ten." By 1917 Hassam's Impressionist sensibility could be seen in his painting *Avenue of the Allies* as well as in other Flag paintings, which celebrated the custom in New York, in the months following the United States' entry into World War I, whereby every allied commissioner who visited the city was given a parade, usually decorated with an abundance of flags.[6] Hassam clearly developed not only an Impressionist style—for example, the green underpainting which mutes the tones of the color, and the development of a fleshy, economical brushstroke—but also the use of an urban scene that likely would have been represented by Pissarro, Monet, or Renoir.

After his first one-person show at the Macbeth Gallery in New York in 1900, Maurice Prendergast associated himself with "The Eight," a group whose membership recognized him as stylistically advanced. The Eight invited Prendergast to exhibit with them at Macbeth's in 1908, along with Robert Henri (their leader and spokesman), John Sloan, William Glackens, George Luks, and others. Although Prendergast was out of place among this crowd, they all shared his feelings regarding European painting, since virtually all of them had been expatriates in Paris—Henri, Sloan, Luks, Lawson, Shinn, and, of course, Prendergast himself. Robert Henri had trained at the Académie Julian (which, unlike the École des Beaux-Arts, had no entrance exam) under the tutelage of William Bouguereau. Nonetheless, by the late 1880s he found himself under the spell of Monet's Impressionism. Upon his eventual return to the United States, Henri began to teach painting and drawing. In 1902 he was hired by the New York School of Art, where he won the allegiance of many of the school's students. Wanting not only to impress him but to retrace his development as an artist, Henri's students traveled to Paris for further education.

Edward Hopper, Patrick Henry Bruce, and Guy Pène du Bois were among those of Henri's students who left the New York School of Art and settled in Paris during 1906 and 1907. Hopper was by far the least interested in making contacts within the Parisian art circles, yet even he was seduced by the ambiance and romance of Paris, which he termed a "paintable city." During this year Hopper began to paint out of doors; his palette lightened and his brushstrokes became tight and broken under the influence of the French Impressionists, whose work he studied at the galleries and salons, and, most importantly, in the Caillebotte collection at the Musée du Luxembourg. Patrick Henry Bruce and his wife were among the first people whom Hopper contacted in France, and it was around this time, in the autumn of 1906, that they first met the Stein family from Baltimore. Gertrude and Leo Stein held salons on Saturday evening to which many artists, both French and American, were invited and which were vital to the education of many young American artists. Hopper did not attend, however, and when asked whom he had met in Paris, he replied, "Nobody. I'd heard of Gertrude Stein, but I don't recall having heard of Picasso at all."[7] Hopper returned to New York in 1907 but spent the spring and summer of both 1909 and 1910 in Europe. The work that he completed during those trips would predict his mature work. In the paintings done along the Seine, for example *Le Quai des Grands Augustins* of 1909, Hopper lightened his palette and used shortened brushstrokes derived from Sisley and Pissarro. The heavy blocks of light and shadow that characterized the work he completed years later in the United States made a more dramatic statement than that found in classic Impressionism.

Gertrude Stein and her brother Leo were important early American collectors of French modernism. They set up housekeeping at 27 rue de Fleurus in the fall of 1903 and, through their Saturday evening salons, became a conduit by which ambitious American painters could learn first-hand the principles of modern painting in Europe. Not only did their salons attract French artists such as Matisse and Picasso, but the Steins themselves amassed a sizable collection of the work of Cézanne, Picasso, Matisse, Renoir, and other French modernists, making 27 rue de Fleurus one of the key locales to see modernist French painting. Leo Stein, much more the theorist than Gertrude, occasionally lent pictures from his collection to American artists so that they might copy directly from French models. While Leo became a major collector of Matisse's work, on the other side of the room his sister collected Picasso's work, and in 1906 brought the two artists together. The other Stein brother, Michael, and his wife Sarah assisted Matisse in opening his own art school, which was attended by many American artists. Before long modern paintings covered the walls of the Steins' atelier, reaching to the very ceiling. This became an incredible resource for visiting Americans seeking to acquaint themselves

JASPER JOHNS
Flag, 1958
Encaustic and
oil on canvas.
41¼ x 60¾ inches

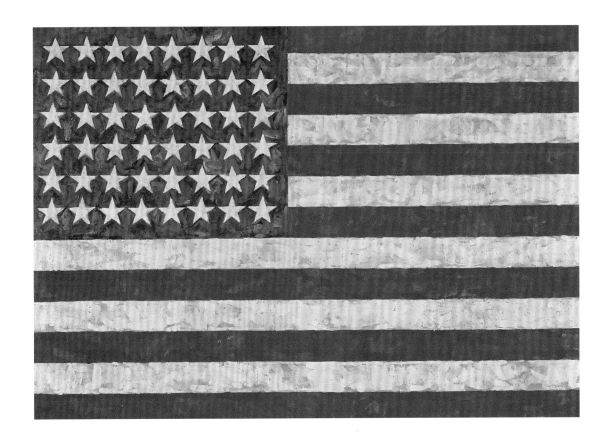

with French modern art. Painters and sculptors as varied as Patrick Henry Bruce, Charles Demuth, Marsden Hartley, Edward Steichen, and Max Weber were in regular attendance, and they assisted their friends—Joseph Stella, Arthur Dove, Alfred Stieglitz, Katherine Dreier, and even Dr. Albert Barnes—in gaining entrance to the Stein salon.

Leo departed in 1913, motivated by disagreements and fights with Gertrude. She then became the central figure of the 27 rue de Fleurus circle as well as an important sustaining presence for American expatriates from both the prewar and postwar periods. When Alfred Stieglitz opened his first gallery, the Little Galleries of the Photo-Secession, or "291" as it was commonly called, in New York in 1908 the work was culled from the Stein circle. Photographer Edward Steichen, then residing in Paris, was a frequent visitor to the Stein salon, from which he developed his knowledge of contemporary French work. He suggested several names of artists to Stieglitz, resulting in the first U.S. exhibitions of Picasso, Cézanne, Rodin, and Matisse.

Gertrude Stein and Stieglitz developed an important relationship, at least on paper, regarding the young American modernists Stieglitz had begun to support. Stieglitz published some of Stein's "word-portraits" in his magazine *Camera Work*, and Marsden Hartley, who first met Stein in 1912, found in her word-portraits an endeavor similar to his own.[8] Many of Stieglitz's artists made their way to Stein's circle at 27 rue de Fleurus, and this important correspondence between Stein and the first American avant-garde artists included Arthur Dove, Charles Demuth, John Marin, and Charles Sheeler. Georgia O'Keeffe never went to Europe, but her education was influenced by both Dove and Sheeler, among others.

The outbreak of war in 1914 made European travel impossible for American artists. Gertrude Stein, visiting England at the time, was not able to return to Paris until after the siege of Paris. The moratorium on civilian travel in France ended in 1920, and tourism increased from 100,000 visitors in 1921 to 400,000 in 1925.[9] In the eyes of the French, the American presence had shifted: the United States was no longer a cultural debtor but rather a participant, an ally. American artists, including Alexander Calder, Stuart Davis, Gerald Murphy, and Man Ray, began once again to pour into Paris. Many of the returning artists from the "291" circle, however, were disappointed to find that Gertrude Stein was largely uninterested in painting any longer, instead concentrating more on her own work and the circle of writers and publishers that had replaced the artists at 27 rue de Fleurus. The one exception seemed to be Stuart Davis, whose *Eggbeater No. 3* of 1927–28 Stein considered buying though ultimately did not.

The most surprising outcome of the aftermath of the war was the degree of pro-American sentiment on the aesthetic front. France seemed to welcome the American expatriates back as eagerly as it did the tourists. America loomed large in the imagination of France during the 1920s as symbols of the machine age, mass media, and popular entertainment appeared in the most advanced of American painting, for example Stuart Davis's *Rue Lippe* of 1928. *Rue Lippe* was not named for a street in Paris

but rather for the Brasserie Lipp, a Paris café. Davis's cubist-inspired canvas was in the tradition of the "poster portraits" popular with members of the Stieglitz circle, especially Charles Demuth, Marsden Hartley, and Georgia O'Keeffe. The picture is a flat-plane cubist composition with a conventional cubist still life inside a streetscape. The portrait refers to Robert Carlton Brown, a poet who lived in Paris at the time; the references to Brown in this word-portrait include the title of one of Brown's books as well as words such as Hotel, Café, Tabac, Suze, and others.[10] Gerald Murphy's precisionist compositions were equally occupied with the themes of consumerism and industrial products, in paintings such as *Razor* of 1924 or *Watch* of 1924–25. Murphy was close to French modernists such as Fernand Léger and Pablo Picasso, who enjoyed his simplified compositions of consumer objects such as match boxes, razors, and fountain pens. Léger and Picasso were frequent guests at Murphy's summer house in Antibes, which the French dubbed the "Villa America." The Antibes house was also frequented by members of the so-called "lost generation" such as Zelda and F. Scott Fitzgerald, Ernest Hemingway, and Cole Porter. Murphy's signboard, set outside the Antibes house, consisted of a painting on board that read *"Villa America"*, and was constructed using gold leaf and tempera paints. It resembled Murphy's machine aesthetic, with its mechanical design of the stars and stripes of the United States flag, creating a simplified abstraction.

French Salon organizations, as well as private dealers such as Paul Rosenberg, openly encouraged American artists to exhibit their work, especially the modernists from the Stieglitz circle. American artists began to waver in their enthusiasm for Paris, however, sensing that things were not quite as exciting there as they once had been. Nor were these artists sure about New York's suitability as a location for an artistic community. As the United States adopted an increasingly isolationist position, so too did these artists increasingly desire a unique American art that was not dependent upon European sources or precedents.

This attitude changed significantly with the advent of World War II. When the Germans occupied France, Americans viewed French art as being held hostage, a damsel in distress. Exhibitions of the work of Renoir and Bouguereau were held to raise money for resistance organizations.[11] American soldiers deployed in France developed an interest in French art and many returned to Europe after the war. Importantly, the G.I. Bill provided a living stipend to veterans and allowed them to enroll in European academies, which they did in large numbers. Painters and sculptors who moved to France on the G.I. Bill found Paris incredibly cheap and hoped to relive the Golden Age of expatriatism. And even though such remnants were nowhere to be found, Americans continued to arrive. The postwar years were an odd time for American artists in France, for New York had begun to assert itself as the center of the commercial art world, and the formation and gradual success of

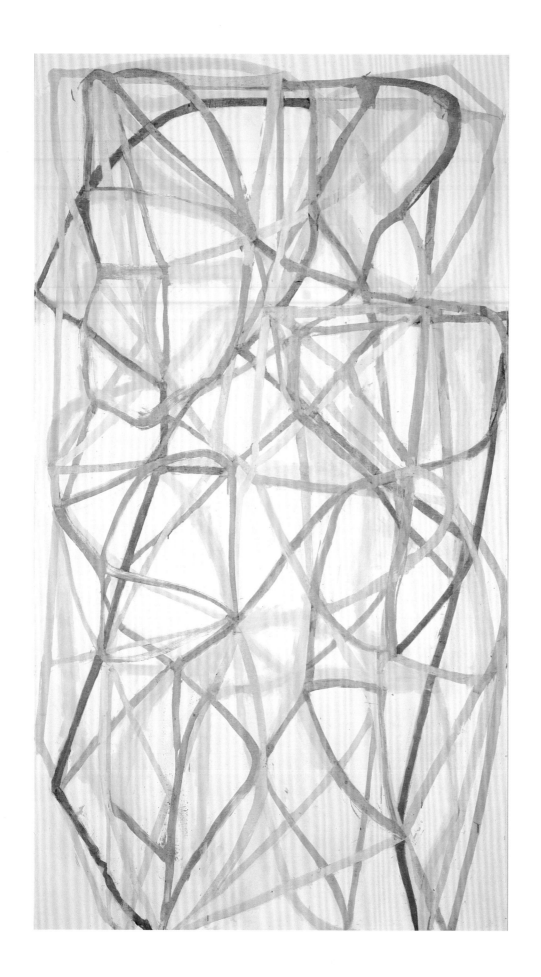

abstract expressionism, including artists such as Jackson Pollock, Willem De Kooning, Mark Rothko, and others, would seem to suggest New York as the most fertile ground for younger artists. Yet one might argue that Paris provided the best environment for American artists to develop their work, away from the tumult that characterized the New York artistic community.

The artists who lived in Paris for a significant period of time after World War II included Beauford Delaney, Sam Francis, Leon Golub, Al Held, Ellsworth Kelly, Joan Mitchell, Nancy Spero, and Jack Youngerman. Americans who spent a year or less included Romare Bearden, John Cage, Kenneth Noland, Jules Olitski, and Robert Rauschenberg. Though this may seem a stylistically disparate group of artists, all emerged in New York around 1956–58 and quickly established reputations and signature styles. This cross-cultural bridge between Paris and New York transported many ideas of the emerging abstract expressionists to the French capital. Equally important is the significant influence— unacknowledged by American critics of the period—of French art on American postwar artistic production (and even sensibility), communicated to the United States through these expatriate artists and through exhibitions of French artists in New York. This generation of American artists, who studied and exhibited in Paris, carried the imprint of contemporary French art and art theory, and when they were later incorporated into the second generation of the New York School no critical attention was given to the significantly international character of their art.

Art critic Clement Greenberg was somewhat responsible for convincing American artists that advanced art required assimilation of the European tradition, and dozens of American artists left for Paris as a result. However, during the ten years that many were abroad, Greenberg shifted his position dramatically with regard to Europe, especially Paris, and proclaimed the supremacy of "American-Type painting." By 1958 interest in Europe had largely abated, and Greenberg became a sort of cultural customs officer, turning back the expatriate Americans who had become "too French." Greenberg did support the work of returning expatriates during the 1960s but he was careful to sweep their European heritage under the carpet. In a 1964 essay entitled "Post Painterly Abstraction," written for an exhibition of the same name at the Los Angeles County Museum of Art, Greenberg articulated the qualities he believed distinguished the younger generation of artists from their predecessors. He included ex-Parisians Sam Francis, Al Held, Ellsworth Kelly, Alexander Liberman, Kenneth Noland, and Jules Olitski, yet took care to point out just how their art was *not* derived from European sources, how "they have not inherited [their skills] from Mondrian, the Bauhaus, Suprematism, or anything else that came before."[12] This reluctance to credit things European continued in Greenberg's writings, and created a palpable tension whenever he wrote about the most "French" of the young Americans, particularly Sam Francis.

Of the postwar expatriates, Ellsworth Kelly and Sam Francis seem to have had the greater success in Paris, exhibiting in Salons and private galleries, and making connections with French artists and critics. During the late 1940s Kelly was acquainted with Brancusi, Jean Arp, and Michel Seuphor, the critical supporter and biographer of Piet Mondrian. By the time Ellsworth Kelly returned to New

York, he had assembled a large group of mature work that was shown at the Betty Parsons Gallery in 1956. Works such as *Fête à Torcy* of 1952 were a curiosity, and many New York critics attempted to align him with the Field painters, such as Barnett Newman and Mark Rothko. However, this was a significant misreading of his work, one that eventually mislabeled him a minimalist. During the six years he spent in Paris, Kelly absorbed many of the formal and intellectual issues that occupied abstract artists during the postwar years, while maintaining his own distinct sensibility and approach to abstraction. American critics had lost their bearings in relation to French art, and did not really know Kelly's sources or recognize the presence of French ideas he had brought to the feet of the New York School. *Fête à Torcy,* in many ways a French picture, was shown in gallery Maeght in 1952. Similar works were shown at the Salon des Réalités Nouvelles in 1950 and 1951. *Fête à Torcy* is composed of two canvas panels that are separated by a black strip of wood. The strange wooden divider declares the painting to be an object (or what Kelly would have called a *tableau-objet* in the late 1940s), thereby removing it from the world of painting alone. This forcefulness of object qualities, coupled with seeming simplicity, is found in much of Kelly's later work, including *Chatham V* of 1971. As the blue and red panels abut, Kelly's painting appears as proceeding from the wall, not as part of it.

Sam Francis fell in with the circle surrounding the critic Georges Duthuit, who was Matisse's son-in-law, almost immediately upon his arrival in Paris in 1950. Through this connection, Francis had

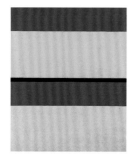

access to some of the most important painting being done in postwar Paris: the cut-outs of Henri Matisse. From his first one-person exhibition in Paris at the Galerie du Dragon in 1952, Sam Francis achieved instant success, both critically and commercially. He sold a painting out of this early show to Madame Matisse, and was rumored to have already exchanged a work with Giacometti. By the mid-1950s his prices matched those of Pollock's in New York. Reviewers compared him to some of the most important contemporary painters in France, in particular Henri Michaux.[13] As his career developed, Francis was considered by Europeans to be the great abstract expressionist, even though he had little or no knowledge of New York School painting except for the work of Rothko and Clyfford Still that he had seen in San Francisco. Francis claimed repeatedly to be motivated by the work of Monet, especially the Water Lilies that had been discovered at Monet's studio in Giverny during the early 1950s. Francis and friends frequently visited the abandoned atelier and examined the large *Nymphéas* panels, which had not been shown for decades. He was not alone in this discovery: Ellsworth Kelly had visited Giverny earlier, as had André Breton and André Masson, among others. It was also in the early 1950s that the Monet cycle at the Orangerie in Paris was reopened after wartime damage had been repaired. In paintings such as *Blue Out of White* of 1958, Francis's careful dissemination of close-valued color across a flat painterly surface was far more redolent to him of Monet's Water Lilies than any work of an abstract expressionist. In this way Sam Francis—and Joan Mitchell—were successful at combining their educations in America with the important traditions of France, becoming, in the nineteenth-century sense, *demi-français,* that is, half-American and half-French.

As the art world became more international in character after the late 1950s, artists moved more freely across boundaries, living and exhibiting in both Paris and New York as well as in other emerging art centers: Los Angeles, London, Milan, and Tokyo. American artists became fascinated with the work of the Nouveaux Réalistes, especially Yves Klein and Jean Tinguely. Jasper Johns had his first Paris exhibitions in 1959 and 1961 at the Galerie Rive Droite after the controversy in New York caused by his flag series. Johns's *Flag*, 1958, though enigmatic in its meaning, relates to the traditional representations of the American flag we have seen throughout the history of American art, including the flags of Childe Hassam and Gerald Murphy. Robert Rauschenberg had two exhibitions in Paris in 1961. After his solo show at Daniel Cordier's, he participated in a group exhibition at the Galerie Iris Clert, where, having forgotten to make a promised portrait of Clert, he presented the now-famous Duchampian telegram that states: "This is a portrait of Iris Clert if I say so.—Robert Rauschenberg."[14] While he was in Paris in 1961, Rauschenberg arranged to secure the theater in the American Embassy for a "concert" in honor of pianist David Tudor. The Embassy refused to allow any advertisement of the concert in advance. Therefore, the concert was performed three days after it was conceived, and nonetheless attracted a large and curious audience. The concert was staged by Rauschenberg, Johns, the French Nouveaux Réaliste Jean Tinguely, and Tinguely's wife, Niki de Saint-Phalle. Saint-Phalle was an American expatriate artist whose role in the performance piece was to shoot a gun from the audience at her white plaster sculpture while Rauschenberg constructed one of his combines[15]—later titled *First Time Painting*[16]—with the easel facing the audience. Tinguely had constructed a self-stripping machine that shed its metal parts as it traversed from one side of the stage to the other. Throughout, Johns was off-stage painting the sign "Entr'Acte" and constructing a beautiful target made of different colored flowers. As the concert concluded, Rauschenberg wrapped his combine in brown paper and removed it from the stage while pianist David Tudor concluded John Cage's "Variations II" on the piano. Johns never appeared on stage and the audience was not allowed to see the combine that had been made.[17]

The ease of international travel and residence has perhaps made "expatriate" category irrelevant. Many artists travel between Europe and the United States with great regularity, including Americans such as Ellsworth Kelly, Barbara Kruger, Richard Serra, Mark di Suvero, and Cy Twombly, to name a

few. Sam Francis kept a studio in Paris until his recent death. Joan Mitchell moved to a country house in Vétheuil, located on the Seine and near Giverny, and lived there from 1959 until her death in 1992, making regular trips to New York where she maintained a studio. Brice Marden lived in Paris in 1964 and since then has visited the city regularly for varying lengths of time. His first exhibition in Paris was in 1969, and his elegant abstractions have captivated his audiences ever since. Marden's *Couplet IV* of 1988–89 is from the artist's Cold Mountain series. In this work Marden has confronted the postwar history of abstraction, even challenging

Pollock's legacy as he assumes a painterly, graphic line that is visually responsible for every inch of the canvas while layers of colored lines intertwine in such a way that there is neither real depth nor flatness but rather a visual vibration that is optically dazzling and very moving. Paris still exerts her seductive influence on younger American artists like Adrienne Farb, resident in Paris since 1978, who achieves in her abstractions a feeling born of color—specifically, the palette of Impressionism—combined with the disciplined linearity of modernist painting.

There has been since the nineteenth century an important artistic dialogue between France and the United States, one that has enriched the cultural lives of both nations. At times the United States has seemed dependent upon the daring and artistic advances of the French; at other times these positions have been reversed. But throughout, the artistic exchange and mutual respect have been constant. This conjoining of artistic concerns has provided a cultural linkage between France and the United States, in which mutual artistic interest (though at times fugitive!) has provided for the vocabulary fundamental to a foundation of visual language or understanding and cultural empathy.

Endnotes

1   Joan Mitchell, interview with Linda Nochlin, 16 April 1986, Archives of American Art, Smithsonian Institution, Washington, D.C.

2   In a letter dated 20 May 1947 Albert Gleizes thanks Rebay for sending food packages and a "marvelous box of shoes and sweaters." Hilla Rebay Archives, Solomon R. Guggenheim Museum, New York.

3   For greater detail on the filming of *An American in Paris*, see Stephen Harvey, *Directed by Vincent Minnelli.* (New York: The Museum of Modern Art and Harper & Row, 1989).

4   Lois Marie Fink, *American Art at the Nineteenth-Century Paris Salons* (Cambridge: Cambridge University Press, 1990), pp. 117–19, 125–26, 132. Fink's study gives an excellent account of the role of American art in the annual Salons, and identifies certain periods of nationalism, between 1810 and 1815, for example, during which wars on the Continent influenced very directly the attitudes toward foreign art, an influence reflected directly in Salon choices.

5   See Sally Webster, *William Morris Hunt* (Cambridge and New York: Cambridge University Press, 1991).

6   *Avenue of the Allies* was previously titled *Flags on the Waldorf,* and the picture was never shown as part of the Flag series. Ilene Susan Fort, *The Flag Paintings of Childe Hassam* (New York: Harry N. Abrams, 1988), pp. 46–51.

7   Gail Levin, *Edward Hopper: An Intimate Biography* (New York: Alfred A. Knopf, 1995), pp. 59–60.

8   See Patricia McDonnell, "Representation in Early American Abstraction: Paradox in the Painting of Marsden Hartley, Stanton MacDonald Wright and Morgan Russell," in *Over Here: Modernism, the First Exile, 1914–1919,* exh. cat. (Providence, R.I.: The David Winton Bell Gallery, Brown University, 1989), pp. 67–75.

9   Elizabeth Hutton Turner, *American Artists in Paris, 1919–1929* (Ann Arbor, Mich.: UMI Research Press, 1988), p. 31.

10   Lowery Stokes Sims et al., *Stuart Davis: American Painter,* exh. cat. (New York: Metropolitan Museum of Art, 1991), p. 198.

11   In the fall of 1941 the Duveen galleries organized an exhibition of eighty-six American-owned pictures by Renoir to benefit for the Free French Relief Committee (an admission of fifty cents was charged). As late as January 1943 Durand-Ruel in New York exhibited William Bougeureau's painting *Nymphs and Satyr,* which had only recently been discovered, and charged twenty-five cents per view to benefit the Fighting French Relief Committee.

12   Clement Greenberg, *Post Painterly Abstraction* (Los Angeles: Los Angeles County Museum of Art, 1964), n.p.

13   Jacques Peuchmaurd, "Sam Francis (Galerie Nina Dausset)," *Arts* 396 (15 February 1952).

14   In 1960 Rauschenberg was introduced to Marcel Duchamp, a heroic figure to the younger artists who emerged in the late 1950s and 1960s. Joshua Taylor et al., *Robert Rauschenberg* (Washington, D.C.: National Collection of Fine Arts, 1976), p. 38.

15   Rauschenberg began to incorporate large objects into his paintings in 1955. These works, which were three-dimensional and sometimes even freestanding, were a combination of painting and sculpture that the artist referred to as "combines" or "combine-paintings."

16   *First Time Painting* was later traded to René Magritte for one of Magritte's oils.

17   The artists considered this concert so successful that when Saint-Phalle and Tinguely visited New York the following year the group decided to perform once again (though Johns bowed out). Feeling the need for more structure, Saint-Phalle approached poet Kenneth Koch about writing a script. The performance piece was eventually titled "The Construction of Boston." See Calvin Tomkins, *Off the Wall: Robert Rasuchenberg and the Art World of Our Time* (New York: Penguin Books, 1981), pp. 192–97.

MARK ROTHKO
White and Orange, 1955
Oil on canvas. 59½ x 49¾ inches

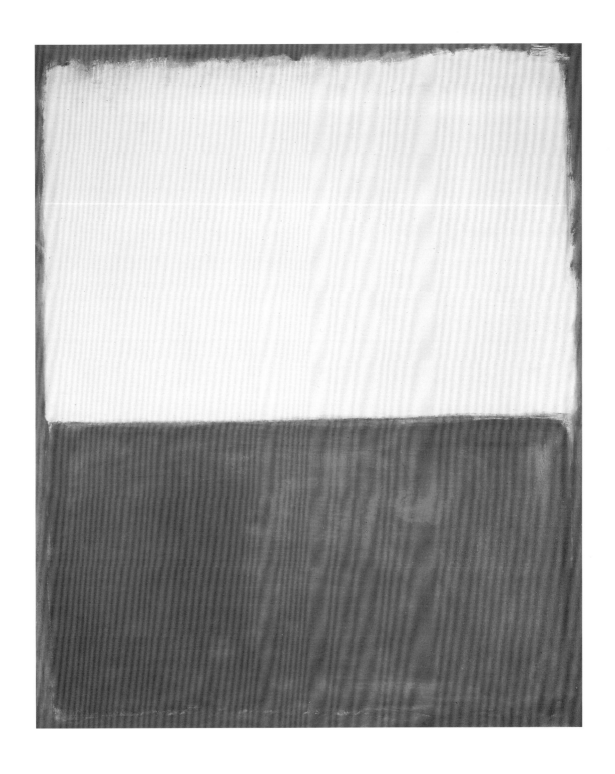

CINDY SHERMAN
Madame de Pompadour (née Poisson), 1991
Limoges Porcelain Tureen.
14½ x 22 x 11¾ inches

CINDY SHERMAN
Madame de Pompadour (née Poisson), 1991
Limoges Porcelain Tea Set; twenty-one piece
tea service, overall dimensions variable

THE STATE DINING ROOM The ornate
panels in this great room were decorated in
1740 by Jean-Baptist Oudry (1686-1755)
and brought from the dining room of
Jacques-Samuel Bernard. The art historian
Verrier wrote that the panels were "executed
with a delicacy that rivals even the Versailles
apartments of Louis XV himself." The U.S.
State Department's Office of Foreign Building
traced the panels to another Rothschild
residence in Boulogne and later purchased
them at auction. After repairs, they were
reinstalled in this Dining Room in 1971.

On the walls hang three enormous Beauvais
tapestries illustrating themes from Homer's
Iliad and *Odyssey*: "The Abduction of
Helen", "The Wrath of Achilles", and
"Venus Wounded by Diomedes".
The designs were made circa 1761
by Jean-Baptiste Deshays.

WILLEM DE KOONING
Untitled XVIII, 1983
Oil on canvas. 80 x 70 inches

THE BALLROOM Once used by the
Luftwaffe as a theatre, the most spacious
room in the east wing has been restored to
its original purpose as a ballroom. Concerts,
lectures, and films are now enjoyed in this
room. A projection room is behind a large
portrait of George Washington painted by
Charles Wilson Peale (1741-1827). Oak
panels in the ballroom, sculpted in 1740 for
the Jacques-Samuel Bernard residence,
show scenes from the *Fables* of Jean de La
Fontaine (1621-1695).

The original paintwork of the Louis xv
panels was stripped during the Rothschild
era, but repainted in 1984. The Belgian
red-marble mantelpiece was originally in the
Samuel Bernard Salon.

LOUISE BOURGEOIS
Untitled, 1947-49
Bronze, No. 1/6.
55 x 12 x 12 inches

LOUISE BOURGEOIS
Corner Piece, 1947- 49
Bronze, AP.
85 x 12 x 12 inches

LOUISE BOURGEOIS
Pillar, 1949-50
Bronze, No. 6/6.
64 x 12 x 12 inches

ACKNOWLEDGEMENTS

The many lenders to this exhibition are gratefully acknowledged for their willingness to part with works that will be missed from their collections. The importance and value of these works made the decision to lend all the more significant. We are grateful to Artes Magnus Inc., New York; Jean-Christophe Castelli; Citibank Art Collections, New York; James Corcoran; the Willem de Kooning Estate and Mitchell-Innes and Nash Gallery, New York; Galerie Karsten Greve, Cologne, Paris, Milano, Karsten Greve, Caroline Messensee, and Martin Guesnet, Directors, Paris; Cassandra Lozano, The Estate of Roy Lichtenstein; The Frances Lehman Loeb Art Center at Vassar College, Poughkeepsie; Matthew Marks Gallery, New York; Robert Miller Gallery, New York; The National Gallery of Art, Washington; The National Museum of American Art, Smithsonian Institution, Washington; The Telfair Museum of Art, Savannah; The Virginia Historical Society, Richmond; The Whitney Museum of American Art, New York, Patsy Blake, Manager, Corporate/Fellows Loan Program; Williams College Museum of Art, Williamstown.

We are indebted to the following artists for their willingness to participate in this exhibition, Louise Bourgeois; Ellsworth Kelly; Jasper Johns; Brice Marden; and Cindy Sherman.

We would also like to thank several people whose advice concerning this project and assistance in securing loans has been invaluable: Leo and Barbara Castelli and Morgan Spangle of Leo Castelli Gallery; Michael Govan, Director, Dia Center for the Arts, New York. Peter Kraus of Ursus Fine Arts and Books, New York, helped to assemble a valuable collection of books on American artists to add to the Embassy Residence Library.

This exhibition could not have been possible without the dedication of the Art in Embassies Program, Washington, D.C, and especially the help of Cohn Drennan, Marcia V. Mayo, Misha Ringland, and Virginia Shore. At the Residence, we would like to thank Robert Mercier, Carla Rosen, and Caroline Pacquement, for their on-site coordination. *The American Ambassador's Residence in Paris*, published in 1997, provided essential details concerning the historic rooms.

We are extremely grateful to Augusto Arbizo and Susannah Rosenstock, Assistant Curators, Jeanne Greenberg Art Advisory, for their research, organization, and hard work on this project.

This catalogue has been greatly enhanced by the original and scholarly contributions of Dr. Robert Rosenblum and Dr. Michael Plante. Thank you to Jack Shear for his impromptu and atmospheric photographs of the installation in progress. The inspired installation photographs were taken with great care by Jacques Dirand and his two assistants, Joseph Dirand and Jean-Stéphane Mus. Thank you to Marie Dabadie for her great assistance in coordinating the photography. Also, for the beautiful catalogue design, thank you to Anthony McCall and his staff.

GEORGES INNES
Lake Albano, Sunset, 1874
Oil on canvas. 30⅛ x 45⁵⁄₁₆ inches
Courtesy of the National Gallery of
Art, Washington, D.C.,
Gift of Alice Dodge in memory of her
father Henry Percival Dodge

CHILDE HASSAM
Avenue of the Allies, 1917
Oil on canvas. 18⅛ x 15⅛ inches
Courtesy of the Telfair Museum of Art,
Savannah, GA, Gift of Elizabeth Millar
Bullard, 1942

MAURICE PRENDERGAST
Beach Scene #4, 1903-06
Oil on panel. 10⅜ x 13⅝ inches
Courtesy of Williams College Museum
of Art, Williamstown, MA, Gift of Mrs.
Charles Prendergast

MAURICE PRENDERGAST
Maine, Blue Hills, 1907-10
Oil on panel. 10⅜ x 13¾ inches
Courtesy of Williams College Museum
of Art, Williamstown, MA, Gift of Mrs.
Charles Prendergast

ARTHUR DOVE
Broome County From the Black Diamond
Oil on canvas. 18¼ x 24 inches
Courtesy of the Frances Lehman Loeb Art
Center, Vassar College, Poughkeepsie, NY,
Bequest of Mrs. Arthur Schwab (Edna
Bryner, class of 1907)

JOSEPH CORNELL
Untitled (Grand Hôtel Bon Port),
circa 1950-59
Mixed media box construction.
18⅞ x 12 x 4⅛ inches
Courtesy of a private collection

EDWARD HOPPER
Le Bistro or The Wine Shop, 1909
Oil on canvas. 23⅜ x 28½ inches
Courtesy of The Whitney Museum
of American Art, NY,
Jospehine N. Hopper Bequest

EDWARD HOPPER
Le Quai des Grands Augustins, 1909
Oil on canvas. 23½ x 28½ inches
Courtesy of The Whitney
Museum of American Art, NY,
Jospehine N. Hopper Bequest

EDWARD HOPPER
Riverboat, 1909
Oil on canvas. 37¹⁵⁄₁₆ x 48⅛ inches
Courtesy of The Whitney Museum
of American Art, NY,
Jospehine N. Hopper Bequest

EDWARD HOPPER
Les Lavoirs à Pont Royal, 1907
Oil on canvas. 23¼ x 28½ inches
Courtesy of The Whitney Museum
of American Art, NY,
Jospehine N. Hopper Bequest

GEORGIA O'KEEFFE
Yellow Calla, 1926
Oil on fiberboard. 9⅜ x 12¾ inches
Courtesy of National Museum of
American Art, Washington, D.C., Gift of the
Woodward Foundation

JACOB LAWRENCE
Library III, 1960
Tempera on board. 29 x 23½ inches
Courtesy of Citibank Art Collection

WILLEM DE KOONING
Untitled XVIII, 1983
Oil on canvas. 80 x 70 inches
Courtesy of the Willem de Kooning Estate
and Mitchell-Innes and Nash Gallery, NY

MARK ROTHKO
Untitled, 1945
Oil on canvas. 19³⁄₁₆ x 25⅛ inches
Courtesy of the National Gallery of Art,
Washington, D.C., Gift of the Mark Rothko
Foundation, Inc.

MARK ROTHKO
White and Orange, 1955
Oil on canvas. 59½ x 49¾ inches
Courtesy of the National Gallery of Art,
Washington, D.C., Gift of Mrs. Paul Mellon,
in honor of the 50th Anniversary of the
National Gallery of Art

JASPER JOHNS
Flag, 1958
Encaustic and oil on canvas.
41¼ x 60¾ inches
Courtesy of Jean-Christophe Castelli

ROY LICHTENSTEIN
Paintings: Picasso Head, 1984
Oil and magna on canvas. 64 x 70 inches
Courtesy of the Estate of Roy Lichtenstein

ELLSWORTH KELLY
Chatham V, 1971
Oil on canvas, two panels. 108 x 99 inches.
Courtesy of the artist

ELLSWORTH KELLY
Fête à Torcy, 1952
Oil on canvas, two panels. 45½ x 38 inches
Courtesy of the artist

JACOB LAWRENCE
Library, 1978
Serigraph, 10⅝ x 15 inches
Courtesy of the Citibank Art Collection, NY

LOUISE BOURGEOIS,
Memling Dawn, 1951
Bronze, No. 6/6. 65 x 15 x 18 inches
Courtesy of the artist and Galerie Karsten
Greve, Cologne, Paris, and Milano

LOUISE BOURGEOIS,
Corner Piece, 1947- 49
Bronze, AP. 85 x 12 x 12 inches
Courtesy of the artist and Galerie Karsten
Greve, Cologne, Paris, and Milano

LOUISE BOURGEOIS,
Pillar, 1949-50
Bronze, No. 6/6. 64 x 12 x 12 inches
Courtesy of the artist and Galerie Karsten
Greve, Cologne, Paris, and Milano

LOUISE BOURGEOIS,
Untitled, 1947-49
Bronze, No. 1/6. 55 x 12 x 12 inches
Courtesy of the Robert Miller Gallery, NY

LOUISE BOURGEOIS,
Untitled, 1949
Ink on paper. 10 x 7¼ inches
Courtesy of Robert Miller Gallery, NY

BRICE MARDEN
Couplet IV, 1988-89
Oil on linen. 108 x 60 inches
Courtesy of the artist and
Matthew Marks Gallery, NY

CINDY SHERMAN
*Madame de Pompadour
(née Poisson),* 1991
Limoges Porcelain Tureen.
14½ x 22 x 11¾ inches
Courtesy of Artes Magnus, NY

CINDY SHERMAN
*Madame de Pompadour
(née Poisson),* 1991
Limoges Porcelain Tea Set; twenty-one
piece tea service, overall dimensions
variable. Courtesy of Artes Magnus, NY

THE ART IN EMBASSIES PROGRAM of the U.S. Department of State was created in 1964 to exhibit original works of art by U.S. artists in the residences of United States Ambassadors worldwide. The residences are the centers for official state functions, and the works of art displayed there serve to support the U.S. Ambassador's mission in that country.

The Art in Embassies Program has achieved its success through lending agreements with museums, institutions, corporations, galleries, individual artists and collectors. All works of art are selected by Program curators who work closely with the Ambassadors to encourage a collection reflecting their interests and vision. Works of art on loan to Art in Embassies serve to provide a visual experience of the cultural and artistic heritage of the United States, while remaining attentive to the host countries' unique cultural and political environments.

The generosity of our lenders makes it possible for the Art in Embassies Program to provide U.S. Ambassadors with excellent and distinctive examples of American art. It is a high priority for Program curators to continually broaden the base of lenders throughout the diverse communities and regions of the country. Art in Embassies'

greatest strength is the support it receives from lenders who become partners with the Program in acknowledging the accomplishments of American visual artists.

Through the Art in Embassies Program and the support of its lenders and donors, thousands of visitors to Ambassador's residences have the opportunity to experience fine examples of American art which encompasses a variety of subject matter and media. U.S. Ambassadors take great pride in these collections of American art and the opportunity for cultural outreach they provide. The Art in Embassies Program is honored to participate in this global effort to support the artistic and cultural accomplishments of American artists.

CREDITS

Published on the occasion of the exhibition AMERICAN ARTISTS IN THE AMERICAN AMBASSADOR'S RESIDENCE IN PARIS at The American Embassy Residence, 41 Rue du Faubourg Saint-Honoré, Paris VIII

Catalogue Copyright © 1998, Jeanne Greenberg Art Advisory

"War and Peace: A Half Century of Franco-American Art Memories" Copyright © 1998, Robert Rosenblum

"From Pilgrimage to the High Life: The American Artist in Paris" Copyright © 1998, Michael Plante

PRINCIPAL INSTALLATION PHOTOGRAPHY AND COVER: Jacques Dirand, Paris.

REPRODUCTION CREDITS:
Page 7: Photograph by Françoise Huguier/RAPHO
Page 11: Copyright © Estate of Roy Lichtenstein
Page 26: Photograph by Eric Pullitzer
Page 30 (top and bottom) and back cover: Photographs by Geoffrey Clements
Page 32: Courtesy of Cheim and Read, NY
Page 36: Collection of Michael and Fiona Scharf, Courtesy of Sotheby's, Inc., NY
Page 37 (top): The Metropolitan Museum of Art, Bequest of Gertrude Stein, 1946. (47.106) Photograph © 1996 The Metropolitan Museum of Art
Page 37 (bottom): Private Collection, Courtesy of Salander-O'Reilly Galleries, Inc., NY
Page 41 (top): The Hirshhorn Museum and Sculpture Garden, Smithsonian Institution, Washington, D.C., Gift of Joseph H. Hirshhorn Foundation, 1966; Photograph by Lee Stalsworth
Page 41 (bottom): The Wadsworth Atheneum, Hartford, CT, Gift of Susan Morse Hilles
Page 45: Photograph by Bob Grove
Page 54: Photographs of installation in progress by Jack Shear
Page 55: Portrait of Ellsworth Kelly by Jack Shear

CATALOG DESIGN:
Anthony McCall Associates, NY